BY MOOREA SEAL

JOURNALS

The 52 Lists Project

52 Lists for Happiness

52 Lists for Togetherness

52 Lists for Calm

52 Lists for Bravery

*My 52 Lists Project: Journaling
Inspiration for Kids!*

STATIONERY

52 Lists Planner

52 Lists Postcards

52 Lists "My Weekly List" Desk Pad

52 Lists "To Do List" Notepad

BOOKS

Make Yourself at Home

THIS BOOK BELONGS TO:

....

....

52 Lists

for

Happiness

WEEKLY JOURNALING
INSPIRATION *for* POSITIVITY,
BALANCE, *and* JOY

BY MOOREA SEAL

Illustrations by Julia Manchik
Photographs by Julia and Yuriy Manchik

SASQUATCH BOOKS
SEATTLE

For my ancestors, and yours

In seeking to create happiness in my own life, I see clearly that honoring those who came before me is crucial to my own healing and contentment. It is a gift to use any resources, be it list-making or therapy, to live a healthier, happier life. I acknowledge and thank my ancestors whose very cells were shaped by their lived experiences, and who live on within me. To cultivate happiness for oneself is a profound pursuit, a breaker of past chains and generational trauma. I trust, with each moment of joy that we manifest, that those who came before us discover new and everlasting joy within themselves, wherever they may be.

For most of my life, I have prioritized so many things over the pursuit of my own happiness. Even the most noble and kind-hearted intentions can sometimes drive us away from the things that ground us and let us thrive. I am someone who believes deeply in investing in the people around me: friends, family, and even strangers. I set enormous goals for myself in my work and fill up my days with lists of tasks for home and the office. But it occurred to me that even when I succeed in the most difficult goals, even when I feel like I've made my community so proud, my own happiness is still not reaching its full potential. I realized that for most of my life, I have pushed happiness to the very bottom of my list of life goals. I have viewed happiness as a possible result of achieving something else, rather than allowing happiness to be the main goal.

It is so easy to forget sometimes that, just like becoming great at playing piano, just like achieving goals in work and tidying up your home, living a happy life takes intention and practice. And you know what you deserve even more than a great job, a beautiful home, or the perfect family? You deserve so much happiness and joy! It's through practicing your own individual pursuit of happiness that you achieve joy and fulfillment in all areas of your life. You are the source of your own happiness, and with weekly practice we can make that happen together! Throughout the year ahead, remember, the root of joy is already inside of you. And by taking the time to contemplate and list what makes you happy (perhaps with your favorite tea by your side and a blanket over your lap), you'll get the incredible experience of connecting to your own deepest self to create a more joyful, balanced, and positive life. Are you ready? Let's get happy!

xo Moorea Seal

Get Together

By picking up this journal, you are already embracing and pursuing joy in your life, and the entire 52 Lists community is waiting in the wings to join you in this incredible experience! This huge group of list makers across the globe is here to support and encourage you along the way as you discover the keys to your own unique happiness. Use the hashtag **#52HappyLists** on social media to discover other people who are working their way through this journal alongside you!

If you'd like even more inspiration for self-investment, personal growth, and lots of fun through list making, check out the **#52Lists** hashtag where friends and fans are talking about what they discover and celebrate through all of their 52 Lists journals!

Would you like to see how else you can become involved in the 52 Lists community across the world? Visit **52ListsProject.com** to learn more!

Contents

Reflect

LIST 1: List what makes you happy right now — 18

LIST 2: List the routines in your personal life and work — 20

LIST 3: List the things that you are really good at — 22

LIST 4: List the things that get you out of your head — 26

LIST 5: List the best choices you have made in your life so far — 28

LIST 6: List the things (from your past and present) that feel like blockades in the way of happiness — 30

LIST 7: List the greatest compliments and encouragement you have ever been given — 32

LIST 8: List the things you like to do that don't involve technology — 34

LIST 9: List all the little things that happened today that brought you joy — 38

LIST 10: List the ways that you feel lucky — 40

LIST 11: List the things that made you happy as a child — 42

LIST 12: List the people who make you feel happy — 44

LIST 13: List the things in your life you are actually able to control — 46

Acknowledge

LIST 14: List everything you feel passionate about   50

LIST 15: List the things you want to say no to   52

LIST 16: List the experiences that have made you feel you are living life to the fullest   54

LIST 17: List the movies, books, and TV shows that make you feel happy   57

LIST 18: List the things about yourself that you *don't* need to change   60

LIST 19: List the ways that you think someone you love would describe you   62

LIST 20: List the happiest people you know   64

LIST 21: List the best opportunities that others have given you throughout your life   66

LIST 22: List the things you prioritize before doing what really makes you happy   69

LIST 23: List the simple ways you enjoy being kind to others   72

LIST 24: List every color you can think of and what mood you associate with each color   74

LIST 25: List the ways that you enjoy investing in your mind, body, and soul   76

LIST 26: List the times when you felt like you made a difference in someone else's life   78

Invest

LIST 27: List your values and beliefs 82

LIST 28: List the projects you have been meaning to work on and finish 84

LIST 29: List the happiest and funniest stories and news you've heard lately 86

LIST 30: List the compliments you want to give to others 88

LIST 31: List the spaces in your life you would like to create more order and organization in 92

LIST 32: List the ways you can "fake it till you make it" in being happy 94

LIST 33: List the people you want to spend more time with before the end of the year 96

LIST 34: List the foods that taste great and make you feel good about yourself when you eat them 98

LIST 35: List the elements of your life where you feel challenged in a positive way 100

LIST 36: List the scents, spaces, textures, and sounds that bring you joy 104

LIST 37: List ten ways to get excited in the next ten minutes 106

LIST 38: List the things you're curious about 108

LIST 39: List the things that you hope will bring you joy this week 110

Transform

LIST 40: List the things that felt important five or ten years ago but are unimportant now — 114

LIST 41: List the ways money *can* buy happiness — 116

LIST 42: List the ways money *cannot* buy happiness — 118

LIST 43: List how where you are right now fulfills dreams and desires of your past — 120

LIST 44: List the gifts you want to give to others through actions, words, and what you can make — 123

LIST 45: List the things, people, and experiences you want to say yes to — 126

LIST 46: List one achievement, big or small, every day this week — 128

LIST 47: List everything that you think of as a treat for yourself — 130

LIST 48: List the things you think you'll want out of life five years from now — 132

LIST 49: List the things you are ready to rid yourself of, things in your home, in your closet, and in your heart — 136

LIST 50: List some images that make you happy — 138

LIST 51: List the ways you have invested in your happiness this year — 140

LIST 52: List the happiest moments of your year — 142

List 1

LIST WHAT MAKES YOU
HAPPY RIGHT NOW

....

....

....

....

....

....

....

....

....

....

....

....

....

....

....

....

....

....

....

....

....

....

....

....

....

....

....

TAKE ACTION: How often do you actually get to experience these things? Just like learning to read, gaining the wisdom and experience of happiness just takes practice. Let's start now! Take one item on your list and see how you can turn it into a daily practice of happiness.

List 2

LIST THE ROUTINES IN YOUR
PERSONAL LIFE AND WORK

....

....

....

....

....

....

....

....

....

....

....

....

....

....

List 3

LIST THE THINGS THAT YOU ARE REALLY GOOD AT

....

....

....

....

....

....

....

....

....

....

....

....

....

....

....

....

....

....

....

....

....

....

....

....

....

....

TAKE ACTION: Underline the things that you had to work for to become good at, and circle the things that you feel come naturally to you. Do any of these things overlap? Just like happiness, it's already within you. It just takes practice to experience daily!

List 4

LIST THE THINGS THAT GET YOU
OUT OF YOUR HEAD

....

....

....

....

....

....

....

....

....

....

....

....

....

....

....

....

....

....

....

....

....

....

....

....

TAKE ACTION: Plan an hour this week to do one or a few of these things that put your mind at peace.

List 5

LIST THE BEST CHOICES YOU
HAVE MADE IN YOUR LIFE SO FAR

....

....

....

....

....

....

....

....

....

....

....

....

....

List 6

LIST THE THINGS (FROM YOUR PAST AND PRESENT)
THAT FEEL LIKE BLOCKADES IN THE WAY OF HAPPINESS

....

....

....

....

....

....

....

....

....

....

....

....

....

....

TAKE ACTION: Look back at List 5 and see if any of your past great decisions can influence how you handle the things that currently stand in the way of your happiness.

List 7

LIST THE GREATEST COMPLIMENTS AND ENCOURAGEMENT YOU HAVE EVER BEEN GIVEN

....

....

....

....

....

....

....

....

....

....

....

....

....

....

TAKE ACTION: Rewrite your favorite compliment on a sheet of paper or print it out in a
font you love. Then tape it to a wall or frame it
in your home so that you are reminded every
day to choose happiness and self-love.

List 8

LIST THE THINGS YOU LIKE TO DO
THAT DON'T INVOLVE TECHNOLOGY

....

....

....

....

....

....

....

....

....

....

....

....

....

....

....

....

....

....

....

....

....

....

....

....

....

....

TAKE ACTION: It's easy to end up spending a lot of time with technology, but does that time really make you happy? Take a half hour each day this week that you would normally spend on screens to do something else that you enjoy. View it as your happiness practice time!

List 9

LIST ALL THE LITTLE THINGS THAT HAPPENED
TODAY THAT BROUGHT YOU JOY

....

....

....

....

....

....

....

....

....

....

....

....

....

....

....

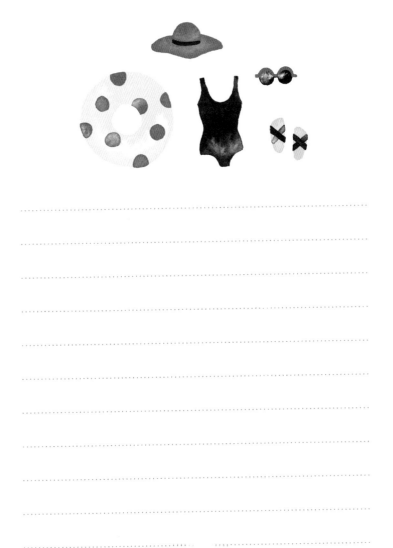

....

....

....

....

....

....

....

....

....

....

....

TAKE ACTION: Every day this week write down one thing that brought you bliss on a little slip of paper, then place them in a jar. Keep this jar of joy going all year, and any time you feel down, dip into the jar to remember the little things that bring you happiness!

List 10

LIST THE WAYS THAT YOU FEEL LUCKY

....

....

....

....

....

....

....

....

....

....

....

....

....

TAKE ACTION: This week hide something special in a secret corner of your neighborhood: place a crystal along a popular path, hide five dollars under a park bench, or leave an encouraging note in a library book for someone to find. Your love will bring them that feeling of luck!

List 11

LIST THE THINGS THAT MADE
YOU HAPPY AS A CHILD

....

....

....

....

....

....

....

....

....

....

....

....

....

....

....

....

....

....

....

....

....

....

....

....

....

....

....

....

TAKE ACTION: Is there anything you used to do as a child that you think you might still enjoy? Pick one thing to try again this week, from rereading a few of your favorite childhood stories to building a pillow fort or kicking a soccer ball around with friends in a park.

List 12

LIST THE PEOPLE WHO MAKE
YOU FEEL HAPPY

....

....

....

....

....

....

....

....

....

....

....

....

....

....

TAKE ACTION: Contemplate what it is about these people that makes you feel so uplifted. Set a date to spend time with or chat with one of them this week.

List 13

LIST THE THINGS IN YOUR LIFE
YOU ARE ACTUALLY ABLE TO CONTROL

....

....

....

....

....

....

....

....

....

....

....

....

....

TAKE ACTION: Cross off anything that involves other people. Ultimately the only things you are going to be able to control are your own actions and choices, and you'll feel better if you can spend less time worrying about the things you can't control. If you feel stressed this week, look at this list and allow your mind to focus on what you can control in a healthy manner rather than what is outside of your control.

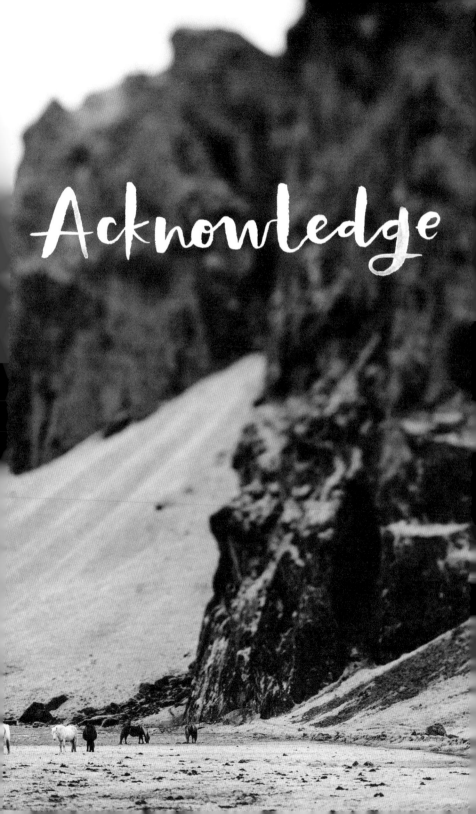

List 14

LIST EVERYTHING YOU FEEL
PASSIONATE ABOUT

....

....

....

....

....

....

....

....

....

....

....

....

....

....

....

....

....

....

....

....

....

....

....

....

....

....

TAKE ACTION: As Van Gogh said, "I would rather die of passion than of boredom." Everyone has a deep-down something that they feel passionate about or desire. Sometimes your passion conflicts with who you think you are or it feels difficult to attain with your busy schedule. Plan an afternoon this month that you will devote to exploring and investing in your deepest passion without fear or embarrassment!

List 15

LIST THE THINGS YOU WANT
TO SAY NO TO

....

....

....

....

....

....

....

....

....

....

TAKE ACTION: Did you include the words *fear* or *guilt* on your list? So often we spend so much time worrying about whether to say yes or no to a person or an experience that we get lost in guilt and worry. It's ironic since the root of having a hard time saying no is that we are afraid of feeling guilty! This week follow your gut and practice saying no to the things you don't have the time, energy, or desire to do. Skip the guilt phase and enjoy feeling assured of your choices!

List 16

LIST THE EXPERIENCES THAT HAVE MADE YOU FEEL YOU ARE LIVING LIFE TO THE FULLEST

TAKE ACTION: Can you take the joy and excitement of these events and re-create them on a smaller scale? If you feel like it's doable, go wild and try one of these things in your everyday life this week.

List 17

LIST THE MOVIES, BOOKS, AND TV SHOWS
THAT MAKE YOU FEEL HAPPY

....

....

....

....

....

....

....

....

....

....

....

....

....

....

TAKE ACTION: Tomorrow morning wake up a half hour earlier than normal and read your favorite book, or watch part of your favorite movie or TV show. It's so much more fun waking up to indulge in what you love than waking up to do tasks!

List 18

LIST THE THINGS ABOUT YOURSELF THAT
YOU *DON'T* NEED TO CHANGE

....

....

....

....

....

....

....

....

....

....

....

....

....

TAKE ACTION: Set a reminder on your phone or calendar to reread this list on this day one year from now to remember all of the ways that you do love yourself and are proud of who you are!

List 19

LIST THE WAYS THAT YOU THINK SOMEONE
YOU LOVE WOULD DESCRIBE YOU

List 20

LIST THE HAPPIEST PEOPLE YOU KNOW

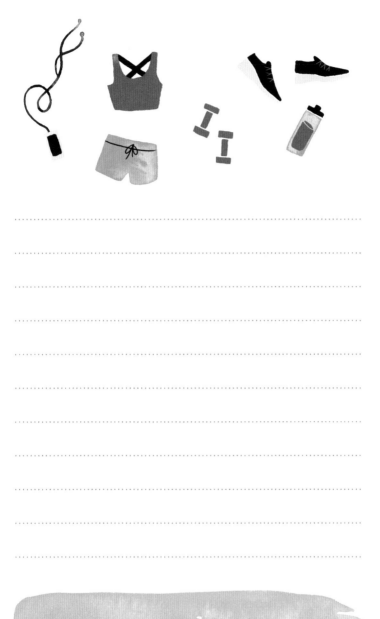

....

....

....

....

....

....

....

....

....

....

TAKE ACTION: How do these people express their happiness? This week try emulating the way that someone you admire expresses their positivity and joy. It might feel uncomfortable or weird at first, but practice makes everything easier!

List 21

LIST THE BEST OPPORTUNITIES THAT OTHERS
HAVE GIVEN YOU THROUGHOUT YOUR LIFE

....

....

....

....

....

....

....

....

....

....

....

....

....

....

....

....

....

....

....

....

....

....

....

....

....

....

TAKE ACTION: Gratefulness is such a huge source of happiness. Write a letter this week thanking one person whose kindness has given you an opportunity to grow.

List 22

LIST THE THINGS YOU PRIORITIZE BEFORE DOING
WHAT REALLY MAKES YOU HAPPY

....

....

....

....

....

....

....

....

....

....

....

....

....

....

....

....

....

....

....

....

....

....

....

....

....

....

....

....

TAKE ACTION: Make a new list with happiness as the number one priority, followed by your other weekly goals and chores. Post this list on your refrigerator. Look at it every day and set the intention of happiness first, then see how you feel at the end of the week!

List 23

LIST THE SIMPLE WAYS YOU ENJOY
BEING KIND TO OTHERS

....

....

....

....

....

....

....

....

....

....

....

....

....

....

TAKE ACTION: Turn this list into a check-list and see how many ways you can be kind to others this week. Mark off each item that you complete!

List 24

LIST EVERY COLOR YOU CAN THINK OF AND
WHAT MOOD YOU ASSOCIATE WITH EACH COLOR

....

....

....

....

....

....

....

....

....

....

TAKE ACTION: Focus on your happiest color this week. Every time you see that color, acknowledge the feeling that it brings you and make it a goal to bring that color into more elements of your favorite space.

List 25

LIST THE WAYS THAT YOU ENJOY INVESTING
IN YOUR MIND, BODY, AND SOUL

....

....

....

....

....

....

....

....

....

....

....

....

....

TAKE ACTION: This week practice one of your favorite ways of investing in yourself for at least fifteen minutes every day. If you're able to get outside while practicing your self-investment on a few of those days, even better! Breathe in that fresh air, soak up the vitamin D from the sun, and feel renewed.

List 26

LIST THE TIMES WHEN YOU FELT LIKE YOU
MADE A DIFFERENCE IN SOMEONE ELSE'S LIFE

....

....

....

....

....

....

....

....

....

....

....

....

....

TAKE ACTION: Take fifteen minutes today to search the news and social media for people who you think are making a difference in the world. How do you want to emulate what they have done within your own world?

List 27

LIST YOUR VALUES AND BELIEFS

List 28

LIST THE PROJECTS YOU HAVE
BEEN MEANING TO WORK ON AND FINISH

....

....

....

....

....

....

....

....

....

....

....

....

....

....

TAKE ACTION: Cross out at least one project that you can let go of for now, then go treat yourself, because letting go is just as much of an accomplishment as starting or completing a project.

List 29

LIST THE HAPPIEST AND FUNNIEST STORIES
AND NEWS YOU'VE HEARD LATELY

....

....

....

....

....

....

....

....

....

....

....

....

....

....

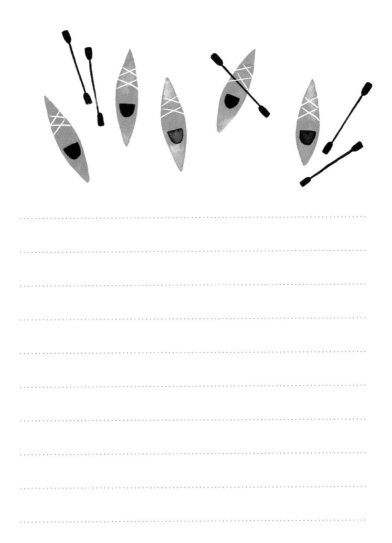

....

....

....

....

....

....

....

....

....

....

TAKE ACTION: Spend time this week with a friend or a group of friends, trading the beautiful and ridiculous stories you have heard lately. It's easy to feel bombarded with negative and heartbreaking news with so much access to information these days. But you have the opportunity to flip the dialogue and fill your time contemplating the positive!

List 30

LIST THE COMPLIMENTS YOU
WANT TO GIVE TO OTHERS

TAKE ACTION: Give one compliment to a stranger you pass by this week. Don't be scared; it's as simple as "What a cute dog!" or "I like your shoes!"

List 31

LIST THE SPACES IN YOUR LIFE YOU WOULD LIKE TO
CREATE MORE ORDER AND ORGANIZATION IN

....

....

....

....

....

....

....

....

....

....

....

....

....

....

....

....

....

....

....

....

....

TAKE ACTION: Focus on purging and reorganizing just one area of your home or office this week: your work desk, your kitchen cupboards, a junk drawer, etc. A clean, organized space is a quick way to get your mind at peace, leaving more room for happiness to enter!

List 32

LIST THE WAYS YOU CAN
"FAKE IT TILL YOU MAKE IT" IN BEING HAPPY

....

....

....

....

....

....

....

....

....

....

....

....

....

....

TAKE ACTION: Happiness and positivity take practice. In practicing self-love I once decided to tell myself out loud everyday that I love myself. And you know what? It worked! Practice saying "I'm happy!" out loud every day this week and see what happens!

List 33

LIST THE PEOPLE YOU WANT TO SPEND MORE
TIME WITH BEFORE THE END OF THE YEAR

List 34

LIST THE FOODS THAT TASTE GREAT AND MAKE
YOU FEEL GOOD ABOUT YOURSELF WHEN YOU EAT THEM

....

....

....

....

....

....

....

....

....

....

....

....

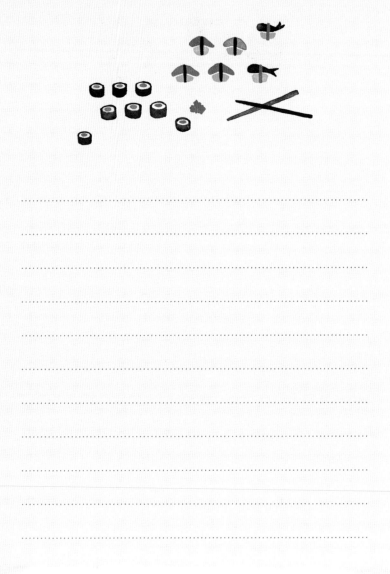

....

....

....

....

....

....

....

....

....

....

....

TAKE ACTION: Time for a yummy snack! Go make or buy yourself a snack that makes you feel great emotionally and physically, and tell yourself out loud, "It's treat time!"

LIST THE ELEMENTS OF YOUR LIFE WHERE
YOU FEEL CHALLENGED IN A POSITIVE WAY

....

....

....

....

....

....

....

....

....

....

....

....

....

....

....

....

....

....

....

....

....

....

....

....

....

....

....

TAKE ACTION: A life without challenges is pretty dull! Sure, life is comfortable without obstacles but then you don't get the chance to discover new paths to happiness. Pick one challenge, big or small, to focus on overcoming this week.

List 36

LIST THE SCENTS, SPACES, TEXTURES, AND
SOUNDS THAT BRING YOU JOY

....

....

....

....

....

....

....

....

....

....

....

....

....

TAKE ACTION: How many of these things can you combine into one joy-filled experience? Try lighting a candle in the coziest spot in your home, pour yourself a glass of your favorite drink, and indulge in some serious me time with your favorite movie, book, or music.

List 37

LIST TEN WAYS TO GET EXCITED
IN THE NEXT TEN MINUTES

....

....

....

....

....

....

....

....

....

....

....

....

....

TAKE ACTION: This is your cheat sheet of ways for you to get positive energy going if you are feeling low and need to get things done! Next time you're feeling low, take a look at this list and take action with one of your favorite positive energy tricks!

List 38

LIST THE THINGS YOU'RE CURIOUS ABOUT

....

....

....

....

....

....

....

....

....

....

....

....

....

TAKE ACTION: A discovery starts with first asking questions and allowing yourself to be curious. Pick one of these interests and allow your curiosity to lead you to new discoveries.

List 39

LIST THE THINGS THAT YOU
HOPE WILL BRING YOU JOY THIS WEEK

....

....

....

....

....

....

....

....

....

....

....

....

....

....

....

....

....

....

....

....

....

....

....

....

....

TAKE ACTION: Review this list at the end of the week, and using the blank list pages in the back of this journal, make a second list describing what moments were actually your happiest. What surprised you in exceeding or changing your expectations of happiness?

transform

List 40

LIST THE THINGS THAT FELT IMPORTANT
FIVE OR TEN YEARS AGO BUT ARE UNIMPORTANT NOW

_____

_____

_____

_____

_____

_____

_____

_____

_____

_____

_____

_____

_____

_____

TAKE ACTION: Phew! Doesn't it feel good to recognize all of the things that just don't matter anymore? Visit FutureMe.org and write yourself an email describing what you hope to not worry about in the future and what you are proud of right now. Set a date to receive it around five years in the future!

List 41

LIST THE WAYS MONEY *CAN* BUY HAPPINESS

....

....

....

....

....

....

....

....

....

....

TAKE ACTION: Give yourself a small budget this week to buy yourself something that makes you feel awesome, whether it's a new book, a spa day, or paying someone else to do a chore that you dislike. Treat yourself!

List 42

LIST THE WAYS MONEY *CANNOT* BUY HAPPINESS

List 43

LIST HOW WHERE YOU ARE RIGHT NOW FULFILLS
DREAMS AND DESIRES OF YOUR PAST

....

....

....

....

....

....

....

....

....

....

....

....

....

....

....

....

....

....

....

....

....

....

TAKE ACTION: What are some other dreams from your past that you would still like to fulfill? Choose one way this week to explore one of your childhood dreams and see how it inspires you!

List 44

LIST THE GIFTS YOU WANT TO GIVE TO OTHERS
THROUGH ACTIONS, WORDS, AND WHAT YOU CAN MAKE

List 45

LIST THE THINGS, PEOPLE, AND EXPERIENCES YOU WANT TO SAY YES TO

_____

_____

_____

_____

_____

_____

_____

_____

_____

_____

_____

_____

TAKE ACTION: Do you ever hold yourself back from an experience that could bring you happiness? Try saying yes to one thing that is a little outside your comfort zone this week and see how it feels.

List 46

LIST ONE ACHIEVEMENT, BIG OR SMALL, EVERY DAY THIS WEEK

....

....

....

....

....

....

....

....

....

....

....

TAKE ACTION: Every achievement is valuable! Take pride in your choices, efforts, and achievements, whether they are as simple as getting out of bed or as complex as solving world hunger. Use the blank list pages in the back of this journal to start a second list of how these achievements make you feel about yourself and your life.

List 47

LIST EVERYTHING THAT YOU THINK OF
AS A TREAT FOR YOURSELF

....

....

....

....

....

....

....

....

....

....

....

....

....

....

....

....

....

....

....

....

....

....

....

....

....

....

....

TAKE ACTION: On little slips of paper, write down all of your favorite treats (whether they are actions, snacks, or activities) and place them in a jar. At the end of each week moving forward, pull out a slip and treat yourself, just because!

List 48

LIST THE THINGS YOU THINK YOU'LL WANT
OUT OF LIFE FIVE YEARS FROM NOW

List 49

LIST THE THINGS YOU ARE READY TO RID YOURSELF OF,
THINGS IN YOUR HOME, IN YOUR CLOSET, AND IN YOUR HEART

....

....

....

....

....

....

....

....

....

....

....

....

....

....

....

....

....

....

....

....

....

....

....

....

....

....

....

....

TAKE ACTION: Let's do it! Pick one thing to get rid of in your home, one thing in your closet, or one thing you've been holding onto emotionally this week. Wherever you start, let it be the symbol for a new beginning of feeling freed from the things that drag you down.

List 50

LIST SOME IMAGES THAT MAKE YOU HAPPY

_____

_____

_____

_____

_____

_____

_____

_____

_____

_____

_____

_____

_____

TAKE ACTION: Create a collection of photographs, drawings, stickers, paint swatches, and anything that puts a smile on your face. Collect these images in a Pinterest board, a folder on your computer, or a scrapbook or notebook.

List 51

LIST THE WAYS YOU HAVE INVESTED
IN YOUR HAPPINESS THIS YEAR

....

....

....

....

....

....

....

....

....

....

....

....

....

Your Last List of the Year!

LIST THE HAPPIEST MOMENTS OF YOUR YEAR

....

....

....

....

....

....

....

....

....

....

TAKE ACTION: You did it! Fifty-two weeks' worth of your truest joy has been discovered, established, harnessed, and cultivated! How many of your happiest moments of this year were things you created on your own? And how many were spontaneous and unexpected? As you look forward into the years ahead, think of this book as your happiness resource. And trust that your life will always hold happiness for you because of two important things: your powerful efforts in the pursuit of happiness and the unpredictable beauty of the world that surrounds you. As hard as life may be at times, there will always be something to spark joy if you seek it. Keep engaging in your own happiness pursuits and embrace the unknown as happiness waits for you around every corner.

MOOREA SEAL is a Seattle-based author, speaker, retailer, and designer, as well as an avid list maker with over one million books, journals, and stationery products in print. Her passion lies in giving voice to the inner child that lives within us all and providing resources for happiness, resiliency, and self-expression. She finds hope in transparency and believes that to truly love and empower others, we must seek to accept and express our own true selves. Join her community at **MooreaSeal.com**.

Printed in China

SASQUATCH BOOKS with colophon is a registered trademark of Penguin Random House LLC

27 26 25 24 23 22   9 8 7 6 5 4 3 2 1

Editor: Hannah Elnan
Production editor: Emma Reh
Cover design: Anna Goldstein
Cover art: Julia Manchik (pattern) and
© 32 pixels / Adobe Stock (paper rectangle)
Interior design: Joyce Hwang
Illustrations and lettering: Julia Manchik
Photographs: Julia and Yuriy Manchik;
page 112–113 © Devon Janse van Rensburg

ISBN: 978-1-63217-475-8

Sasquatch Books | 1325 Fourth Ave, Suite 1025 | Seattle, WA 98101

SasquatchBooks.com